Life Stuff

Life Stuff

Poems by

Rose Mary Boehm

© 2023 Rose Mary Boehm. All rights reserved.
This material may not be reproduced in any form, published,
reprinted, recorded, performed, broadcast,
rewritten or redistributed without
the explicit permission of Rose Mary Boehm.
All such actions are strictly prohibited by law.

Cover art by Lorette C. Luzajic, artist and poet extraordinaire
Cover design by Shay Culligan
Author photo by Rose Mary Boehm

ISBN: 978-1-63980-466-5

Kelsay Books
502 South 1040 East, A-119
American Fork, Utah 84003
Kelsaybooks.com

For Alfonso and Pascale with love and gratitude.

Acknowledgments

Thank you so much to the following publications, where versions of these poems previously appeared:

Alkhemia Poetica: "Leaving Home"
As It Ought to Be: "Discontent," "Sirocco," "Cumbrian Summer"
Atrium (UK): "My Friend in Meth"
Crossways: "Somewhere, Moontime"
Cyberwit Press: "Another Spring"
Galway Review: "I Love Paris," "When It's All Over," "Portent"
Impspired: "Notes from the Margins," "The First Time I Saw Black," "Recipe for Wellness"
Loch Raven Review: "Inflection Points," "My Brother," "Letter to Angst," "Recipe for Wellness," "Comfort from the Birds"
Lothlorien Poetry Review: "Aum Manu Padme Hum," "Bodies," "Driving Back from Prague," "Snow," "Compostela Was Once Called the Field of Stars," "A Good Day for Love in Madrid," "My Ghosts," "Evensong," "Some of My Rains," "Letter to My Best Friend" "A Question of Belonging," "Letters from Paris," "My Grandfather," "Past and Future," "A White Sheet of Paper," "Embers," "Yin and Yang," "Advent," "Feierabend"
Misfit Magazine: "Sunsets on Mars Are Blue," "Damage Control,"
Naugatuck River Review: "I Find the Healing Fairy in an Old Suitcase"
Off Course: "How to Prepare for My Final Flight," "Foxtrott," "Invisible Arms Around My Neck," "Friday Night Binge in the City of London," "Old Knowledge," "Music"
Poeming Pidgeon: "The Chulel"
Poetry Super Highway: "Sharp Joy—Soft-Edged Memories"
Pure Slush: "Coming Home," "Sighting of the Unicorn"
Pyrokinection: "Counting Sheep," "Sweet Ghetto," "I Always Loved You, Life"
RAR (Rat's Ass Review): "Not Staying for Lunch," "Spurned"
Red Eft: "Guilt"

Shark Reef: "Nightcall"
Silverbirch: "A Memory"
Sky Island Journal: "Blue"
The Poet's Touchstone: "Nobody at This Address," "About Bread, Germany (1944)"
Verse Virtual: "I Am Tired of Being Tired," "Should You Not Recognize Me, How Could I Explain Myself to You?" "Flatlining During the Operation," "Gravity," "Mining in Spain," "An Evening in One of London's Inner Suburbs," "A Summer's Day," "A Nop-Time," "I Wonder," "Where Poems Live," "Tumble," "What Doesn't Kill You," "Far Away from Cell Phone Antennae," "Waltz Me Towards the Tango"
Writing in a Woman's Voice: "Apple Crumble with Love," "Bless the Broken Things," "On the Cusp"

Author Note

I have reached the last installment of my life and can't help thinking about the various components that make up the many years I have lived through ups and downs—as we all are wont to do. Many of these thoughts have become poems. Here they are in part I.

In part II, I offer you a random collection of memories and musings, poems about "stuff that comes to mind" when you start thinking too much.

Contents

I.

Embers	19
I Always Loved You, Life	20
A Memory	21
Apple Crumble with Love	22
Advent	23
About Bread, Germany, 1944	24
What I Learned When I Was Six	25
Another Spring	27
The Moment a Lightbulb Goes Off in Your Head	28
The 'Good' Old Days	30
Crossing Illegally from Germany into Germany	31
Glamour	33
Nobody at This Address	35
Perhaps None of This Ever Happened	37
Notes from the Margins	38
Foxtrot	39
The School Reunion	40
Inadequacy	41
Musings	42
Invisible Arms Around My Neck	43
My Brother	44
Barry White was Droning from the Tape Machine . . .	45
A Summer's Day	47
An Evening in One of London's Inner Suburbs	48
Guilt	50
Before we Had Cell Phones	51
Past and Future	52
My Grandfather	53
The First Time I Saw Black	55
I Love Paris	57

Letters from Paris: 1958	58
Inflection Points	60
Sirocco	62
A Question of Belonging	63
Not Staying for Lunch	64
Driving Back from Prague	65
Leaving Home	67
A Good Day for Love in Madrid	68
Evensong	70
I Find the Healing Fairy in an Old Suitcase	71
Mining in Spain	73
Flatlining During the Operation . . .	75
Compostela Was Once Called the Field of Stars	77
Snow	78
My Ghosts	80
Some of my Rains	81
Sharp Joy—Soft-Edged Memories	83
Feierabend	88

II.

Coming Home	91
Bodies	93
Finding Out Where I Belong	94
Waltz Me Towards the Tango	96
Sweet Ghetto	98
Family Reunions	100
I didn't	101
Discontent	103
Damage Control	104
Friends	105
Counting Sheep	106
Aum Manu Padme Hum	107

Should You Not Recognize Me, How Could I Explain Myself to You?	109
The Day I Stopped Reading the News	110
Music	111
Gravity	113
I Am Tired of Being Tired	114
How to Prepare for My Final Flight	115
Remembering Where I Came From	117
A White Sheet of Paper	118
Bless the Broken Things	119
A No-Time	121
Blue	122
I Wonder	123
Friday Night Binge in the City of London	124
Cumbrian Summer	125
Letter to Angst	126
Spurned	127
When It's All Over	128
Where Poems Live	129
Yin and Yang	130
time somewhere	131
urban wilderness	132
Recipe for Wellness	133
Sighting of the Unicorn	134
Somewhere, Moon Time	135
On the Cusp	138
The Magic of the Word, or the Blind Girl Reads Braille	139
Old Knowledge	140
no way out	141
Nightcall	142
My Friend in Meth	143
Portent	144

The Chulel*	145
The Prophet's Vision	146
Sunsets on Mars Are Blue	147
Tumble	148
What Doesn't Kill You . . .	150
Comfort from the Birds	152
Far Away from Cell Phone Antennae	153

I.

Embers

I live in the embers of fires
that once were fierce. White, gold,
red, amber conflagration.

Youth.
Needs must.
No prisoners.
No forethought.
No consequences considered, torching
what came near enough, and the iceman a chimera
whispered about by shivering old women

no longer strong enough to hold the flames.
I have felt his breath in the shadows.
Last night he held my hand, sightless, unforgiving.

I Always Loved You, Life

You have showered me in riches. You have hurt me beyond
measure. But I am getting tired now. I started the battle
early, and the warrior woman's arm is lowering her bow.

I wore a coat of many colours, became what the world
wanted me to be. Claimed my freedom by melting
into walls. Sometimes you could see the fissures.
I did what I needed to do in the anonymity of plain sight.

I lusted after the steppes of my mother's forebears,
my long mane blowing in the wind.
My DNA remembered that I honoured the goddess,
cared for the land, herded, and told the stories of old.

Didn't know what it means to belong.
But I always was a quick learner,
my deceit well practiced.
You never quite found me out as not of your pack.

A Memory

The way my father stood
by the evening sun-lit window, a golden halo
playing around his hair
and how he would look
so quietly out of the window, blinking
into those slanted rays of burnt orange.

His thumb in his waistcoat pocket,
his watch chain performing
the perfect shape, just as watch chains
hanging from waistcoat pockets
should. Rather than seeing it then,
I knew that on the left side
of my father's nose
there was a fleshy mound—not too big.
I would always recognize
my father's nose.

I couldn't see that either,
but I knew my father's hat
hung on the stand-up wardrobe
in the hall, the one with the big mirror
and the large hooks made from a copper alloy,
doubled so as not to damage the clothes. I was tracing
the raised flower pattern on the wallpaper.

The evening sun slants across my desk
and makes it difficult to see
the computer screen. My eyes
are wet. The insistent phone calls me.

Apple Crumble with Love

I didn't know about grown-up desperation
then. Had got used to carrots, potatoes, and water.
Didn't mind porridge made with wheat ground in Mum's lap
with our old coffee grinder. Had no idea what coffee was.
I knew whey, not milk. Butter was a foreign word.
There was something nice in a slice of dark bread
with a layer of mashed potatoes. Sometimes
I brought home an egg, stolen, still warm,
from under one of Frau Keller's hens.

For my birthday Mum made an apple crumble
with flower, water, and a few apples which
had overwintered in a drawer, wrapped
in newspaper. At the time I didn't understand
why Mum was crying when she tried to
prize the beautiful apple crumble from
the baking tray with a hammer and a chisel.

Advent

During the War, we made a wreath
with fresh pine twigs. Four candles.
We always had candles because
the lights failed often, a power station
bombed perhaps. You never knew.

For the Advent wreath we needed
fat red ones, but white ones would do.
And I was allowed to light each one,
one every Advent Sunday, until
there were four, and Christmas
was only a second away.

I had an old Advent calendar from 'before',
before I was even born. Some of the little
paper doors had already given in to use.
I knew the pictures behind them
by heart and yet looked forward to seeing
them again. Old friends. A promise
of wonders to come.

And there was little Baby Jesus, and his mum,
and the donkeys, camels, sheep,
the shepherds and the star.
My uncle had whittled a crib for me.

One day the miracle became a story
like any other.

About Bread, Germany, 1944

I can see myself. A small girl. White vest, black, ballooning
shorts, handmade. She stands on a milestone, giving her the height
to overlook the wheatfield, trying to see the wave.
In the distance a cuckoo calls.

The children have finished picking out the
potato beetles and their larvae by turning over each leaf,
walking slowly through the field where row after row
of the potato green thrives, ready for August. I see the girl
in front of the big farmer's wife, her apron a sea of colours,
here and there slightly soiled. The woman presses
the big round loaf against her swelling belly,
cuts it in half and hands the child a slice as long
as two of her hands after spreading some lard.

The girl is walking home from the bakery.
The baker lady cut out two coupons from the ration
card. Under the child's left arm, a big, crusty loaf.
With her right hand, and an experienced finger, she hollows
the bread through the crust from the exposed end.
At this moment she doesn't think about consequences.

They picked up the last wheat from farmer Braun's
field after he finished the harvesting. Mother
carried it home in a bag she'd brought. Left the stalks
to dry on the windowsill, beat out the grains.
She sits, the coffee mill between her legs,
her dress sagging between her thighs.

If we find enough firewood, we'll have
a small fresh loaf tomorrow.
If the train doesn't get bombed,
Father will arrive just in time.

What I Learned When I Was Six

My first death was the sow.
I'd held her in my arms when she'd been small,
how heavy she had seemed.
That wriggling, fat, slippery body.

I kissed her on her little snout with the black dot,
her funny feet scratched me in her scramble
before she slipped back into the muddy straw,
falling into the wriggly mass of pink and grey bodies,
seeking her mother.
We called her Irma.

After about six months (for six-year-old me
that was 'a long time later')
I heard a cry so piercing that I felt it cut my bones.
Standing on tiptoes, I looked from the kitchen window
and saw big Irma in the yard, four men holding her legs,
the executioner sliding his knife
across her throat from ear to ear, her mouth reminding
me of Guernica—looking back with adult eyes—
and soon her throat was a gaping, open wound.
The knife was rather small, I thought,
for doing so much damage.

There was the blood.
Liters of blood.
From our kitchen window
I saw Irma's body drained and then
hacked
into
pieces
by old men wielding big knives and even axes.
A bucket full of her blood
taken to the utility outbuilding.

I am not so sure, now, at the end
of my life, but I think I understood then
what the grownups meant when they
talked about the war deaths in hushed voices.

Another Spring

In those last days, boys in uniform
came past the house where mothers
would fit them out with their own son's trousers
and shirts —the weather had turned mild.

In those last days I didn't sleep a child's
sleep. We'd shuffle to the shelter
that smelled of cool earth, moisture
and things growing on wet walls, settle

into the night counting the seconds, minutes
from the first droning. We waited
for deafening obliteration. I shivered
and crept further into my blanket

when we heard the bombs make contact,
the staccato of strafing fighter planes—
the *Flak* had long since made a vow of silence—
and boys using bazookas

on anything that moved.
On one of those last days my brother
pushed his teddy between my praying hands
and I found solace in worn tufts of wool.

The Moment a Lightbulb Goes Off in Your Head

I remember that long, long road on which I walked
to the train station. Thoughtful and elated.
A road I knew so well but this time it was endless.
Every time I looked ahead, the station
seemed as far away as it had been
before I set out.

The last time I'd seen him and felt his arms
lifting me up was eons ago. I had been little then.
Now I was grown up. I was eight!
Would he recognize me?
Would I recognize him?

In the station yard, some people were sitting, waiting.
Mother had given me some Pfennige (pennies)
for a platform ticket.
More people were milling there.
The train was not due for another ten minutes,
but trains just came when they could.

I saw the steam before the train.
People hanging from doors, sitting
on any available little platform or footplate.
Some on the roof.

As people streamed off the train and filled the tiny platform
I felt very lost and near to tears. I had never scanned faces
so thoroughly and quickly. One last old man walked out
to the other side of the barrier.
There was no one else.

And I stood there and grew up.
The train slowly puffed away,
forcing itself onto the long climb up into the hills.

As the last carriage passed, I looked across the railway lines.
And he was there.
His trench coat, his hat, suitcase in hand,
smiling at me and walking across the rails.
He jumped onto the platform and looked at me.

I did not move. I stared in shock—and then it was easy.
It no longer mattered.
What had just happened was irreversible.

When my father died, I was far away.
I managed to be at the funeral.
I managed a tear or two.
I felt loss and the loneliness
of being shoved onto the front lines.
I wondered why I was empty.

Just now I understood:
I had done my mourning when I was eight.

The 'Good' Old Days

In the summer I walked barefoot to school.
I had no shoes. Sometimes we had 'klapperle',
sandals made from wood that 'bit' your sole
near your toes when the leather that covered
the hinges had worn away. But my feet
had hardened during that long autumn,
when we ran through the stubble
left by the harvesters of wheat, rye, and oats.

In the winter we'd use the skis that our wheelwright
made. 'Lift your arm to measure the length'.

Our landlord had chickens. Sometimes I was allowed
to go and fetch an egg. Still warm and not too clean.
Sometimes, in the spring, I would play with the baby goats.

Sometimes I didn't know how to explain the holes
in my homework. Paper almost punched out.
I'd left my budgie alone for a moment.
Mother bent over the sewing machine.

The worst days were the days of butchering.
The pig's cry almost human.

That spring morning when the radio said that
the war was over, that Germany had capitulated,
that the American Forces where coming in,
that spring morning when the jeeps and planes
'parked' on the new, green shoots
that had been our food.

Crossing Illegally from Germany into Germany

At seven I walked that long road
past farmer Bauer's geese, left at the church,
left again at the brook, over the small bridge,
past the school caretaker with his scary grin
to take my seat
with the local kids.
I, the refugee.
I, the one with the strange accent.
'Heil Hitler!'

My teacher had hairy legs
and big calf muscles that went in and out,
up and down as she biked along the school path.
I stared.

Under the bridge, by the brook,
I found my friend the frog and stroked
his slimy head, his whole little body seeming
to breathe in and out fast and in panic,
but it stayed, hypnotized
by my gentle finger.

The cockerel waited by the shed. I tucked him
in under the tiny blanket of my dolls' pram.
I covered his comb with a little blue hat
my mother had crocheted
for my doll,
his wattles fell to one side,
his protective membrane closed.

The street names changed
to Marx, Engels, Lenin . . .
I received the coveted blue scarf,
became a Young Pioneer.

The teacher with the big, yellow teeth
taught me Russian.
Mother decided that this was enough.

In the train chugging towards the border
my attention was on Mother.
I looked at my brother.
In the wooded copse I rested my head
on the backpack I'd dropped
onto a patch of woodruff.
It also smelled of ceps.
I thought of Grandpa.
I sensed danger when Mother said
to wait for darkness.

The soldiers unfolded from the night,
standing on the higher ground, silhouetted against
the starry night sky.
The clicks of their safety catches.
Even though my brother had finally
given me his Teddy, I peed myself.

Glamour

Aunt Lil wore her black hat at a coquettish angle,
its little veil pulled over her forehead.
She was Arpège and blood-red lipstick,
long, pointed fingernails to match, nylon stockings,
everything I wanted to be one day.
She bought me 'Schillerlocken'.*

My uncle was a lawyer,
a tall tree in a forest of lesser trees.
He seldom bent down to my ten-year-old,
somewhat undernourished body.
With a stentorian voice he hinted
that I was making a nuisance of myself
just by being a kid.
I found out later that he had always thought
my mother a creature of a lesser race.
She didn't speak like one is used to hearing.

It was whispered behind fluttering hands
that Aunt Lil had been a barmaid.
Now she was the wife of a professional,
was perfume and lace, and a deep-red slit
replaced her mouth when she laughed.
Which she didn't do often.

The idea that this childless couple would look after me
for ten days while my mother went back
to East Germany (in danger of being sent to a Russian
gulag if caught) to sort out the lives we left behind in a hurry
had been hammered out between the women.

Uncle Fried looked at me across the huge dining table
as he would a fly and frowned.
'Has nobody shown you how to eat
with knife and fork, child?'
My voice not quite steady from fear:
'We had nothing to cut, Uncle'.

---

* "Schillerlocken" is **a sweet, cone-shaped German pastry**. The name was inspired by the typical curly wigs that men, like the German poet Friedrich Schiller, used to wear in the 18th century."

Nobody at This Address

I left of my own free will, smelling the blood
of a big world that waited just for me.
Perhaps I was used to moving, used to being
of no fixed address. But that's not true either.

We had, for years, and then more years,
fixed addresses. We just didn't get to keep them.
More and more bombing raids. Neighbours
buried under the rubble, a huge hole
in the field where we'd played.
The house opposite was still quietly burning.

We left for a place where my mother was born,
where I had aunts, grandparents, a flat I thought
a palace, where my mother had to fetch the water
from the pump, and where I collected warm, dirty eggs
from underneath brown chickens.

Then the horizon was on fire. More conventional
bombs were dropped on Dresden and more
destruction rained from the sky than on
Hiroshima and Nagasaki only six months later.
One day soon after we hung out the white sheet.
Surrender.

And two armies marched. And marched.
German women and girls preferred the current
of the river Elbe to being trapped by the Russian army.
And when it was all over, we returned to what was
left of the other home which I barely remembered.

After some years of change I endeavoured to find
my own Silk Road, to taste exotic flavours, to survive
without help from those who loved me. Then they all
took Charon's boat too soon, and I was too far to see them off.

But I will burden my children with these stories
only if they ask.

Perhaps None of This Ever Happened

Can't find the place
where we buried the cockerel.
Sometimes I can still hear the rabbit's
high-pitched scream.

There was that boy who asked
for a kiss and I said no.
Embarrassed he ripped off some
grass. He had short pudgy hands
with bitten fingernails.

In the town on which I'd turned my back
we'd planted trees. For a long while
they stood there, thin, and unassuming.
Sixty years later they hide my youth.

Notes from the Margins

I

His swaps came down the rows
of desks through many grubby hands
until they reached me. And on each one
(a shiny basket full of forget-me-nots, a chubby angel
leaning on a cloud, or a rose tied with a silver bow)
he had written in his very best, I love you.
He was fourteen to my almost twelve.

II

I found a poem in the bottom of my aunt's
sewing kit, the aunt who never married, the one
we thought of as 'the spinster'. The poem
talked about love. Scribbled in the margins
in my aunt's tidy hand I could make out,
'Darling man, if only my father weren't so needy'.

III

Between what a 12-year-old took for love
and my aunt's self-denial,
I find marginalia wafting in and out
of view, a touch here, an abandonment
there, or a happy merengue danced
on the tiny floor of an intimate bar
somewhere in Minga Guazú.

Foxtrot

Giggles behind clammy hands,
starched skirt, five petticoats.
Only this morning 'they'—
on the other side of the hall—
wore short pants and dirty faces.
Yesterday I beat them at math,
apart from the volleyball that
nearly killed Werner.
We were worried but had to giggle.
He was always such a prat.
Today they are stiff
in their Sunday best, and with their
awkward stance they've become ETs.
Some are still drifting.
The teacher is at her shrill,
most schoolmistress best:
"Boys to the right, girls to the left.
Choose your partners.
Foxtrot please, band . . ."

The School Reunion

It had been 50 years. There are moments I remember, of course, there always are. Helga's mum had cigarettes. She kept extra packets in the drawers of her kitchen cabinet. Our faces soon had a green sheen, and there was, I recall, a distinct need to retch. There was Manfred who rode his bike next to mine and showed off his hands-free skills, no matter where we went . . . quadrivial and more. There was Werner who limped. I always had a weak spot for creatures who weren't perfect. I looked at them all after 50 years and wondered what made them so old. We smiled and tried to catch up. Children, grandchildren, stories told by people who once couldn't cope with calculus or didn't know where you'd find the Hudson Bay. Quite a few weren't there at all.

White-capped waters
vast deltas the end of land—
peace of the deep

Inadequacy

When I moved to that village
with my mum they convinced me
that I didn't belong.

When I returned home after many years
the kids on the street and in school
made me understand that I didn't belong.

There was no money. Mum sewed
my clothes by hand and Singer.
The other kids laughed.

My best friend's family had too much money,
her mother dressed her in expensive
grown-up clothes. The other kids sneered.

When I was nineteen, an elegant woman
looked me over and curled her lips when
a handsome man showed interest.

I worked hard, earned well, dressed better,
surprised when men wanted me.

I married, had children, made new friends.
Then the neighbour called over the fence:
Your cat just pissed on my lettuce,
you stupid bitch.

My husband cheated on me.
Of course, I thought.

At ninety I opened the old photo album.
All I could find was a gorgeous young woman
with beautiful children.

Musings

My mirror. Registering time,
reflecting place. Telling reverse truths.
Somewhere in my backroom a picture.

Her face engraved on the palimpsest of my mind.
In parallel universes, the ones where memories
live, did I ever make it out?

This boy. His hair fell over one eye,
and he blew it back with a well-practiced gesture. I think
he became a butcher. He'll never be older than fourteen.
His name was William, I think.

My second child is the third. I wouldn't
miss her for the world, but I do ache
for the one who changed her mind.

One day my mother could barely walk, and her cheeks
gave in to gravity. My grandmother, forever wearing a black beret,
a network of wrinkles covering her face.

Our fiftieth school reunion.
They had all become old people.

Invisible Arms Around My Neck

Never really got to know you because
you left too early. Never saw you,
except with my heart's eyes. Still,
I loved you as I did the others. And ever since
I began to bleed, you've been with me,
in my heart, in my flesh. I will always
think of you as my second child.

My Brother

It's not easy to be sixteen with a kid sister of eight.
You get shtick for that from your friends, especially
if you love her enough to make her kites and things
and teach her to skate on Ruttenberger's frozen pond.

Later I came from wherever I could—by plane, helicopter,
train, by Fiat Cinquecento crawling up from Munich for 800 km,
or passing the border between Holland and Germany
with my vicious cat firmly locked into its travelling basket.

Long walks. Long beers. Restaurants, bars, and cafés
all over the once thriving harbour, now a fashionable haven
for those of us who had the time. The holocaust monument,
the bike lanes, windy terraces, his tall, slightly bent
frame walking with steps that made me feel small again.

We sat at the canoe club, in a weak sun,
our collars up against an imaginary wind.
Kids at the mini pier laughing and mucking
about. He told me then, and there rose a silence
between us. We slowly finished our beers.

I still visit. They packed his ashes with earth
and seedlings. He is growing into a tall and slender birch,
fresh young branches reaching for the sky.

Barry White was Droning from the Tape Machine . . .

. . . when my Cinquecento bit the dust.
Well, not quite. It had some life left.

Almost nine months, popping even my maternity dress,
I somehow pushed the little car
to the side of the main road.

I knew how hippos feel. Couldn't even see my shoes.
That kind man interrupted my thoughts.

That kind man was also huge—
He'd stopped his pick-up truck. Came over.

"Where's your husband?
He should be flailed, letting you drive
in this condition."
What 'condition'? I was pregnant.

Not the time to get feministy.
He got a toolbox from his truck,
lifted the engine hood, twiddled some wires, fixed it.

The greengrocer watched from behind his counter,
his customers had a field day.

The big man looked me over one more time, sighed.
At my husband's 'incompetence'?

Then he smiled, picked up his toolbox, walked off
shaking his head. Wanted no pay.
A knight in a dirty overall.

Getting behind the steering wheel was quite a squeeze.
Hippos are not meant to drive Cinquecentos.

It had all been a bit of a rush.
Met in August,
moved in together in October,
my furniture followed me in November,
married December,
pregnant in January.
Now was the end of another September.
Love conquers all, doesn't it?

I decided to hang the new curtains.
As I stood on that ladder, I did not know
that soon a girlfriend would be asking
for my husband's hand in marriage.

A Summer's Day

The seagulls reclaim their rocks after we pick up kids, buckets, shovels, towels, and assorted wet bathing suits. The evening sun finds the sand still glued to salt-water sticky faces. Small diamonds on their noses. Hair wet and lank, their perfect little bodies tanned from the Cornish sun with a bite in high summer. The wind picks up.

Three kids in the tub
Exhausted mothers stretch out—
The perfect day

An Evening in One of London's Inner Suburbs

A soft splash in the pond, the moon trying
to rise above the sycamores that have grown
too large for back gardens. They hold her with their
green, leafy fingers, a prisoner in their crowns.
There is still a faintly glowing horizon. The sun
is loath to give up his dominion to the wool-headed
moon who spins dreams and stories half remembered,
leading us astray with the glorious possibility
of painting outside of all lines.

The mosquitos have come out to play, too close for comfort.
I can see them, tiny wings glimmering in the first
moonlight that steals its way through the sycamores.
Another splash in the pond, a dog's soft howl
in a garden beyond, the cat slinking through the hole
in the fence, just next to the little door we kept
for our small children to visit the neighbours, our friends.

I can hear Queen's 'Bohemian Rhapsody' across
the park-like square where all the gardens meet,
possibly coming from the open back doors
of the young percussionist, a tiny young woman
I met when we were both out walking
the dogs. She said she came to London with 'The Who'.
Hers a mighty, kindly mastiff, mine a flirty licorice allsorts.

Thinking of little Miss Muffet.
Why do the vets shave the spot
and sterilize it before they plunge in the deadly poison?
I wipe my eyes. No, I am not crying for the dog.
I am crying for the end of a love that was supposed
to last until 'death us do part'.
Will he have me put down?
He did say that me wanting to leave was probably

due to a hormone imbalance while menopausal.
Do the kids know that Melinda is not a friend?
The evening continues to wind its serenity around
my sadness. I am moving gently on the swing we made
for the kids when they were little. They are out partying,
making music, flirting, trying out their new adulthood.

I shall just have to make sure their cars are home
when I wake up in the early morning hours.

Guilt

They said, "We are going to meet a friend.
her family died in a Concentration Camp."

"Are you nuts?" I said, "You want her
to meet me, your German friend?"

"We'll ask," they said.
They asked. "Yes," she said.

I went.
It was a Sunday in Holland.
It was in the big old hotel.
Huge columns of old marble
that looked like freshly cut meatloaf.

A small, old woman, slightly bent, white hair,
her legs forming an inverted triangle.

She is slowly walking towards us, looking at me.
She stretches out her arms, her open hands.

Before we Had Cell Phones

I

I nearly fall out of bed. The sharp shrill
of the phone. Again. Gawd, it's two in the morning.
Mum, I missed the Tube. Half blind I find my jeans, pull on
a sweater. Where the hell are my keys. Look with a certain
resentment at her father who is snoring gently.
How on earth did I negotiate those tortuous bends
half asleep. Just the thought makes me shiver.

II

Now they have their own cars. Decided
not to fret and take a pill instead. Nothing
good can come from not sleeping. First light
finds me peering through a gap
in the curtains. His blue one? Parked. Her little
red one? It's on the other side of the road.
Of course, it's under that tree from which the birds
will carelessly deposit their droppings.

III

Forty years have passed. Crossing Marylebone High,
my daughter takes my elbow, matches my stride,
releases me only after depositing
me safely on the pavement.

Past and Future

The past takes on a rosy sheen. Thinking
of my childhood in a world war, I rarely remember
death raining on my city, blown out windows,
the stench of burning flesh, the years of separation
from my father when he 'abandoned' me.

There was the breeze made visible by the wave
of the wheatfield, the finer points of a slug,
delight in a hairy little caterpillar, and the hares
zigzagging across the frozen field at the back of fence.
Skiing to school during a white winter, or walking
barefoot, leaving footprints in the asphalt softened
by a burning summer sun. The geese in farmer Braun's field
to be feared, the worry: will Mum have managed
to swap the box of silverware against
a sack of potatoes?

About growing up I ought to remember
unkind comments on my home-made clothes,
dwelling on my as yet non-existent breasts,
deciding to leave my art for fear of ridicule.
And one day I was about to die from bleeding.
Mother said I was a woman now.

My past has been a long one
and memory is a tricksy friend.

Two children, two grandchildren. May they find
the wave of the wheatfield in a summer's breeze.

My Grandfather

He taught me the colours of the jay whose ungainly voice
jarred in the quiet of the glen, when the coocoo allowed
competition in her endless showing off, having laid her giant egg
in the red-breasted Nuthatch's nest.

Insects buzzed, dizzy in the shafts of sunlight that forced
their brilliance through the bright green leaves
of the deciduous trees mixed into the evergreen spruces,
conifers and firs. Our feet sunk into the soft, rotted carcasses
of fallen trees already covered by beds of moss.
An unforgettable scent emanated from open wood wounds,
mold, mildew and endless thick layers of built up ur-forest
that teamed with life: beetles, ants, worms, centipedes and,
of course, mycelia, the trees' internet, blabbermouth
and keeper of secrets.

In the autumn we hunted in the dark, wet, secret places
after the rains. He knew them all and sniffed them out:
boletus, chestnuts, umbrella mushrooms, birch mushrooms,
chanterelles. Watch out for the baddies. Some are obvious,
showing off their poison proudly like the red cap, others
try to dress and appear like everyone else. Make sure
you recognize them by their small give-away misses.

He presented me to his bees. Of course, I had delighted
in the stolen sweetness in his house. On the occasional piece
of bread, and secretly sticking my not too clean finger
into that golden stickiness and licking it. Slowly.
My grandfather approached his small friends without protection.
Some alighted on his shirt sleeves and shoulders.

Hello, my girls, he said. At first, I kept my distance,
not quite trusting they would recognize their giant soul mate's
granddaughter. But as he checked on the honeycomb,
the deep super frames, I approached better to observe,
and as I stood in awe, those hard-working, furry pollinators,
with wings too short for their bodies, danced on my naked arms.

Now, at the end of my life, the gift I bear for my grandchildren
is the poison chalice of the destruction of their world.

The First Time I Saw Black

And they were very, very black.
Tall, elegant, and black.
My friend and I, newbies in Paris, 18 and wide-eyed.
We were sophisticated Parisians, sitting in a café
on the Left Bank. *La rive gauche.*
People watching. What else?
She from Sweden, I from Germany.
We had met at the Sorbonne,
measuring the size of the world.
Susanne had a Vermouth; I had a Dubonnet.
It tasted like poison, but the ads were irresistible,
and if you wanted to pass for international grown-up,
you said it out loud, pronounced it just so.
To the gorgeous waiter who smiled.
He couldn't have been much older than we were.
Oh, and his French . . . *Mais oui!*
And then they walked by. Slowly.
Seemed to be looking
for a table.
We passed each other as we were leaving.
I think we gaped.
At that moment the dynamic changed.
Instead of sitting down where we had just left,
those two handsome guys
accompanied us to the bridge.
Leaning over the sides of the bridge, looking into
the dark waters of the river Seine,
we made conversation haltingly, our French
at an embryo stage. *Comment ça va?*
Those two were fluent, but had an accent we hadn't
heard before. The whites of their shirt collars emphasized
the black of the skin of their necks and faces;
when they smiled, we saw a row of white
gleaming in the streetlights that lined the bridge.

Well, you know.
The usual.
D'où venez-vous?
Where are you from?
It's been so long; I think they came from Senegal.
I don't know about my friend,
but as we stood there and tried our wings,
one of the Senegalese boys put his hand on the bridge stones
next to mine.
My hand so white.
His hand so black.
We looked at each other and marvelled,
our hearts growing in the knowledge that the world
was indeed a wondrous place.

I Love Paris

We can't write about the moon.
It's been done.
To death.

Can we still mention soft summer nights
pierced by the cicadas' insistent
call for sex? The smell of wet earth—
is it still acceptable in a poem?

And worse—to come full circle—
we used to visit Paris April . . . May,
when blossoms tumbled, loosened by sharp
spring winds and it delighted us with architecture,
eclairs, Les Deux Magots, and the horse-drawn
carriage in which we used to hold
hands in the Bois de Boulogne.

Letters from Paris: 1958

I

My first week in Paris. Damn it,
my French stayed behind somewhere
between college and Walburg, Hesselberger
& Frankenveldt. At least
I remembered how to call a porter
when I got off the Express from Düsseldorf
at seven in the morning.

Wonder if Mum's over the shock
that I'd prefer this cauldron of sin
over a secure typing job
at the local lawyers. She's like a chicken
that's hatched a duck's egg:
hysterically running up and down
the lake shore watching the chick swim.

II

In the *Gare St. Lazare* where I have to take
the train to the *Banlieue* (the suburbs
for you and me) this pretty Arab boy
was trying to chat me up.
Here I am, Elfriede from Werter Street,
crossing *Pont Neuf*, looking up at *Notre Dame*,
walking around *Place de la Concorde,*
sitting in *Les Deux Magots.*
If they could see me now.

Went to the movies. One of the double-bill
was 'Cat on the Hot Tin Roof' in English.
French subtitles. No English, no French.

Had to make up the dialogue.
Elizabeth Taylor was gorgeous, as always.
Paul Newman angry most of the time
or sulking. He probably said to her:
'You piss me off no end'. And she:
'Get rid of that stick and I show you'.

III

Somebody tried to sell
the *Tours Eiffel*. I have nobody
to talk to, *mon Dieu*.
But I'm breathing the same air—
give or take a few car exhausts—
as Talleyrand, Cardinal Richelieu
and *Les Trois Mousquetaires*.
On the *Champs Elysées*
I passed some handsome *flics*
who whistled when I went by.
Mother wrote. She's coming Monday
to take me home.

Inflection Points

Back again. Every time we touch down at Nice
I have to dig out my *français,* and I become a different person.
More *je ne sais quoi,* more Gallic perhaps?
I begin to move my hands when I speak, shrug my shoulders . . .
donc, c'est extraodinaire, n'est-ce pas? Strange, wouldn't you say?

We commandeer a table for five in our favourite watering hole
in the old town of Antibes.
We had planned for Biot, that extra-special
restaurant with its *omelette aux truffes,* the truffle omelette
to die for. But our friends could only make it to Antibes,
and so we meet again at Le Bouchon; the night is warm,
the noises gentle and very French,
and the wafting garlic mixes with the yasmin,
oleander, and pines into something you never forget,
a smell unique to the *Côte.* It will accompany you
in less opulent days and remind you of those moments
when your evenings were full of laughter, and the bottles
of wine too small. *Passe-moi le pain, s'il te plaît.*
Pass the bread, please.

'Comandeering a table' meant for the waiters to pull
three small tables together and arrange chairs around
the little eating island newly created with good will
and in the name of enjoyment.
There were five of us.

Mark would soon move on to Thailand to join his
husband to be. They were going to open a fashion empire.
Jean was going to take over the branch in Miami (he sighed).
We teased him about leaving civilization behind.
Gina was about to retire. She wasn't sure whether
she might stay in France or simply travel the world.

We may never see Alison again. She had been diagnosed with MS and wasn't in a good place.

As I took another sip of my Côte Rôtie, I knew my life had yet again arrived at an inflection point.

Sirocco

The hot winds blow northwards.
Labouring hearts adapt to a slow-burning rhythm.
Nights find you breathing harder,
dreaming languid dreams dipped in Saharan orange.
Snow melts into puddles, makes
little rapids in the gullies.

Shy bright green unfolds on hitherto
barren winter stalks, like young girls
succumbing to the whispered promise
of swelter, not heeding either calendar
or caution. Cars covered in red sand
use the roads like go-cart runs. An early
tulip pushes through heavy slush,
a sense of unseemliness in the air.

On a park bench two grey heads,
woolen scarves undone daringly,
galoshes protecting warm shoes.
Old hands stripped of thick gloves,
he holds hers and bends over them as far
as his stiff back gives him leave.
The Sirocco will hold a few days.

A Question of Belonging

Where are you from? they ask,
and I can't tell. The more urgent
their enquiry, the less
I understand the question.

My mind contemplates
geographies and deeper places
excavated by fear, love, desires,
and the grand fugue.

I pulled in my roots a lifetime ago.
They now hang suspended in mid-air,
needing nothing more than
an affable welcome.

Not Staying for Lunch

Walking up that hill
near the Cypriot village
where Dimitris' mother was born,
we had to pause often, out of breath.
The old, shrivelled Maria—nobody knew
her real age—black dress, black apron,
black scarf, who had seen her family
go one by one, came towards us,
light as a goat, almost skipping
alongside us those last twenty meters.
When she kissed me, I shivered.
Her watery eyes almost disappeared
under sagging lids, her mouth
had fallen into itself, her smile
a black hole. Dimitris' head
buried between her sagging breasts
for a moment of remembrance.
A brown chicken hurried past
but not fast enough to escape
Maria's nimble move and firm grip.
The chicken's neck in her hand
she asked us, 'You stay for lunch?'
Dimitris shook his head.
Maria fingers opened.

Driving Back from Prague

I

Monsters used to live in me,
behind pillars, planning
ambushes in every dark corner.

II

We drive through Eastern Europe's
endless woods, where fables breed,
and Hänsel and Gretel wander still.

Wolves. Bears. The car devours
black asphalt. In the headlights
grey motes, the windscreen
fills with small cadavers.

No yellow lines.
No street lights.
No-one.
The blackness blackens.
The trees close in.

Orange lights.
Military men.
The border post.

III

I remember another border,
another night, when safety catches clicked
in quick succession.

IV

The bleak monster is a little man
in a greatcoat, collar up.

He wields
a red stamp.
Next . . .

Leaving Home

The next morning we'd have to take the ferry
from Dover. The next morning I'd have to say
goodbye to my kids. The next morning
could wait.

In the old Cornwall pub,
Newcastle Steam Beer flowed freely, and Paula
fell in love with Paul. Not that anything happened,
mind you. It was just a spark that made
the hairs on my arms stand up.
Paul had a girlfriend,
Paula a husband.

The next morning was far away. But, eventually,
they called 'Time'. And we all moseyed off.
Paula and I to my car. We had to get to London that
night. The next morning . . . oh, well, you've heard
that one by now. Heavy, a little drunk, and my heart in knots,
I made it from Cornwall to London in just over
three hours on angel wings, consciously not exceeding
the speed limit for fear they may stop me
and smell the Newcastle Steam Beer.

We got to my house.
We fell into our beds.
We slept.

We had all the stuff ready to go, and the morning
happened, that's what mornings do. We loaded
the car, I didn't see much.
I don't remember whether the kids
let me kiss them. I hope they did.
I think I waved goodbye.

A Good Day for Love in Madrid

We curved and cursed
along new motorways,
wrong exits and eccentric
signposts. They'd hidden
that place where my old van
would be inspected for
roadworthiness and get that
coveted sticker 'to be
displayed at all times'.

We finally got to sit
on those hot silver aluminium
chairs under the trees
on the *Alcalá*. 'Two beers
and two *gaspachos, por favor.*
Make sure they're cold'. High noon
on the Castilian plateau.
The thermometer painted by Dali.

You had come half-way around
the world to seek me, you said.
Those ice-cold Spanish beers
I'd thought more likely. A study
in amber and frosted opaque.
For a nano moment our hands
stuck to the glass.

Life became good again
under that ancient Acacia.
The occasional car hissed by
on the softening asphalt.
Aliens in air-conditioned tin cans.
Darkened windows closed.

There are no monkeys in Madrid's
Acacias, I think. Still, aimed with precision,
a viscous projectile splashed into my
soup from somewhere up high
in the canopy of leaves. From
shock to helpless laughter
I arpeggioed the full register
of emotions an ice-cold
gazpacho produces when it
splatters against your hot face,
sloshes all over your best whites,
and drenches your hair,
lavishly coiffed to impress the
potential lover.

I swear I heard a snicker
in that tree, and when I'd
wiped my eyes I saw your mirth
and fell for you.

Evensong

When I met you that day between the tall building
at the corner of Argensola and Santa Barbara
I marvelled at your beauty.
Your ebony hair danced on the evening breeze.
Your back curved under the blue silk shirt
that tried to follow its seaward line.

We walked at your rhythm,
dreading separation, we pressed on through the crowds
in the old part of town . . . in calle de León we found
a table for one-and-a-half, and the sweet odour
of your skin was stronger than the clouds
of black tobacco lingering blue against the yellow lights.

You wanted only to dance. Life didn't suit you.
You said you hadn't asked for it so why
had it chosen you?
Your hands touched mine.

My love's back curves convex, his hips' hinges rusted.
I smile at the white wisps of remaining wave.
You hadn't wanted a job in admin,
but write poems that make my toes curl.

I Find the Healing Fairy in an Old Suitcase

It grew for 14 years he said.
14 years of sleepless nights, pain, love, laughter, good health,
the time in a woman's life when so many delete
us from the records.

Fusili frutti di mare in our favourite Italian,
the critics' screening of 'Midnight Express',
the première of 'Superman',
seeing and being seen in 'San Lorenzo's
in London's Beauchamps Place,
hanging up the washing in the garden,
picking the kids up from school,
the other mums worried about lice,
something not meant for the well-heeled.

Dad lunching with a young woman
whose long, dark, curly hair hid her face.
He didn't see me sitting a couple of tables to the right.
He only had eyes for HER . . .

My son wants his birth certificate. He is 16,
his latest girlfriend is 24. She suggested they get married.
My daughter's first boyfriend, she sneaked him in for the night.

It's been eight years since Dad's lover
broke through the magic circle I'd had painted
around all of us with imaginary chalk.

Many MacDonald's and Pizza Hut's later,
we have supper in the same favourite Italian restaurant.
I explain why I must leave for a while.
It's hard to find the words,
and we grow silent.
Look at our plates.

Many miles from what had been home,
the headaches start. The fever.
Meningioma, he says. Benign. But the operation
may seriously affect your motor skills.
'Then again, she may not make it',
he says, almost to himself.

They all rally around. Fly in. The ones I left,
the new friends, my old love, my new love. My daughter
gives me a healing fairy: long stripey legs, big grin, small, floppy
wings.
The kind of wings that don't get you off the ground.
The surgeon hangs it on the bedpost
when they wheel me into the operating theatre.

12 hours later I can hear their laughter and know
that I've been forgiven.

Mining in Spain

Waves of aches,
dwarves hammering in my head,
whistling while they work.
Fever and nausea.
Meningioma, señora.

It's a healing fairy, my daughter smiles under tears.
Long dangling stripey legs.
Wings too small to fly,
the bumble bees' dilemma.
My kids,
my ex,
my now,
my boss,
my friends—
all rooting for me in the clinic's café,
cracking jokes.

While they dig for my hammering dwarves
on the operating table, I go on field trips.
Then I flatline.
That must have been the moment
when I realized that death does not exist.
It's just stepping over the line.

Later I absented myself again
when my head weighed at least a ton,
the size of a Pilates ball.
Just pulled in my feelers, played dead.

But you can't keep it up. Eventually
the stuff they give you wears off.
Pain. It almost makes you scream—
But you know it's not done.

My love is smothering my face with moisturizer.
He holds me tight, walks behind me.
One step at a time old girl,
don't worry, we'll get there.

Flatlining During the Operation . . .

Where the river Styx meets the shore,
where Charon's boat lies for anchor,
where I stepped off the vessel
returning to where I was so unceremoniously
bundled into the lower decks,
I saw.

I had inner compound eyes and the sharpness
of an eagle. I looked down at the topography
of my life and saw rivers turning back
onto themselves, sinkholes of life's random
disasters, enormous canyons
carved out of dissatisfaction,
gentle lakes of passing beauty taken over
by poisonous algae, deserts from droughts
I had inflicted on a once verdant landscape.

There were the Himalayas of my expectations,
the Andes of my most joyful moments,
the Alpes where I searched for
the mystical blue flower.
And then I knew.

That search had created the limitation
of my geography. I had hunted the unattainable
while fields lay fallow, weeds conquered all,
small houses and enormous constructions crumbled,
the sheep and cows—skeletons of negligence,
species I hadn't even known lived in me—extinct.

The world could have been mine while
I idled, doubted, sowed out empty seeds,
procrastinated at great speed.

When I returned from the Underworld,
I threw open the borders, righted the rivers,
mowed the meadows, vanquished the weeds,
and strapped on the wings I hadn't yet used
for fear of falling.

Compostela Was Once Called the Field of Stars

Starting in St. Jean de Pied
we walked about 20 km, with 780 km
to go. To the centre of the greater
pilgrimages.

St. James of Compostela, legend
and shard of transcendent truths.
Take the route of the Milky Way,
he said to Charlemagne.

Occasional sharp morning light
flows over us under the tall trees
of the Pyrenees. Our pace slows.
Pass the water bottles. The cheerless

dirt roads along open fields
seem relentless. 40 more days
at this pace. I hoped it would, but
the hand of God hovers nowhere.

Snow

It hadn't snowed at the appointed time.
The peaks of the Pyrenees stood slate grey
and barren. Off-white and shredded,
snow blankets barely covered the lower slopes.
Stringy ghosts, Baqueira's ski lifts, like clockworks,
moved in their pre-ordained paths, the tiny
seats solemnly nodding only to each other.

Defrauded, those huge stiff boots you'd think
are for the surface of the moon, skis and sticks
leaned with a melancholic air against the
wooden partition between changing rooms.
Some fashionable all-in-ones passed under
the half-open window, heads flicking carefully
coiffed manes, mouths twittering with added
zeal. After all, one was here to be seen.
The bars were full.

What started as a flurried dance that night, not sure
where up was or where down, anon took weight
and clear direction. 'Down!' was the inaudible cry,
followed by: 'Spread out!' Impossibly white,
cloud-loads of powdery snow descended
and soon camouflaged the world we knew.

When it was over, bar a few stragglers here
or there pirouetting slowly onto an absurdly
pristine shroud, our host said: 'Vamos, amigos!
Dress in your warmest.'

The cold moon, hung in cloudless black,
made our shadows ominous, they snaked
over mounds and into hollows ahead of us
and difficult to follow. That prodigious white stuff
restrained our progress.

Just when we thought we'd rather die
than take another aching step, we had arrived.
And 24 huskies, 12 to each sleigh,
were lying on moonlit and bejewelled white,
harnessed, ready, expectant, keen. Even today
I'd swear they had been grinning.

We cruised across the high plateau at speed,
the dogs, like bullets from a gun,
streamed across the shadowed white.

A spell had spun a web across our words.
The stars had dropped towards us and
we heard their tiny voices pealing
across the void.

Some light years later we returned
and woke from our trance.
The dogs released were calm and
sweated from their tongues, while
the champagne froze in the plastic flutes.

My Ghosts

Our old house in the middle of nowhere.
The downwind is filling the air with woodsmoke.
From under the eaves something dark uncurls,
insubstantial, adding a smell of moss and wet earth,
memories of a burial ground perhaps.
I am not good at funerals.

In the posh urbanization, the housekeeper's son
drowned in the unsecured pool. He'd been three.
Why would they care about a kid that's not theirs?
His small, naked feet leave watermarks on the ground floor.
I am not a good companion for dead children.

Our new home on the other side of the world.
In the dark I feel cold and the touch of invisible tendrils.
I can feel a woman, and she's begging for attention.
Someone told me that they killed her in the entrance.
Her cry on my skin.
I am not a good companion for ghosts.

Preparing the table for lunch, two unseen hands
are lightly pressing on mine, and I remember.
Not putting the napkins straight was my ex's pet peeve.
Now that I think of you, you make me laugh.
The one thing you always did best.

Some of my Rains

Warm rain in the Caribbean,
giant bathtub abruptly
turned over by a tropical giant.
Rain that hurts. Rain that washes
away topsoil, flattening crab claw,
golden trumpet and scorpion orchid,
leaving the wax rose gasping for air,
fills all dents in every hotel patio.
Tennis courts become square lakes
of reddish, sandy mud. Every passing
car's a drencher. Take off your sandals.
Let your feet transmit the moment
when a god created water and land.
A stifling thirty-eight degrees in the shade,
sabotaged for a brief, exulted moment,
soon reclaims its protagonism.

A dry spell on the Castilian plateau. Earth
crust breaks like freshly baked bread. All greens
from spring and early summer dusted ashen
by hot winds. The sky turns a metallic grey,
eucalyptus whisper urgent messages to
the poplars who bow deeply in acquiescence.
Fat drops explode on the patio roof, cut through the
pines, leave welts on the soil. Soon the rains break.
The world smells of summer
and wounded earth.

Squishing from the soggy wooden terrace
to the overflowing frog pond. Grasses bend
under the weight of the constant drizzle
of an English summer. Brushing past the dripping
hollyhock, it shakes its droplets onto my hair.

Peony's heads hang low, the song thrush
shelters in the blackthorn. The shed's rusted
door hinges whine. From my poisonous-orange
slicker dried earth from last year is washing off.
Into sudden silence the song thrush trills
an acknowledgement of a forgotten afternoon sun.

In the Peruvian coastal desert people know the
word 'rain'. Sometimes a Lima cloud forgets its
miserliness and spits a little water.
Worn stone gets slippery.

Sharp Joy—Soft-Edged Memories

1

Making approximate noises to the Baroque trumpet concierto,
with a voice that once had the clarity of bells. I know
every note, of course. Unexpected winter sun streaming
into the kitchen, the trumpet at full blast. Fillet steaks.
Broccoli cream. A bit of onion perhaps, one potato.

I move my head to the irresistible rhythm and conduct,
knife in hand, ready to dissect the garlic. Someone shouts from
a window across the yard to another person I cannot see,
'No te olvides la mascarilla'. 'Don't forget the mask'.
It is COVID time in Lima, Peru. Plates, bowls, taste . . .
The top of the waves of the Pacific sparkle.

2

I only once owned a coveted open top. But it's summer
in Madrid, and all car windows are open. The tape machine
works again, and Callas wonders whether 'He's the one'.
La Traviata one of my favourite operas. Callas' voice is beginning
to wobble. Navacerrada, pines from somewhere below reaching
into the heavens. I am immortal as long as no car comes
towards us on the hairpin curves. We are going up, up, up.
There is this restaurant I know in Sepulveda's Plaza Mayor.
After lunch we'll mosey down to the Duraton
to visit the *gallinazos*.

3

Took the kids to school, it's a gentle, sunny London morning.
Washing ready to be hung, I carry the basket onto the lawn.
Nothing smells quite as wholesome as wind- and sun-dried
linen. From the open window Mungo Jerry.
I move my hips; my arms, hang the washing to the beat.
Just may pull out the deck chair and get some tan
in-between the rapidly passing white puffy clouds
that, for uncomfortable moments, make me shiver.
In the summertime . . .

4

An inspired sun has dried the wet leaves and the muddy paths
in the park. My bedroom windows wide open. A summer breeze
moves the curtains. Vivaldi. Winter. It'll have to do.
Making the beds. It's Sunday morning in Den Haag.
There is a scent in the air of sea and some sweet flowers.
A quick *uitsmijter.* Nothing elaborate.
Rob will arrive soon. He said 20 minutes. Sailing on Aalsmeer.
All day.
Rucksack: *Jenever.* Beer. *Broodjes.* And in that order.

5

Circumnavigating the Starnberger See in my Fiat Cinquecento.
The car has two luxuries: an open roof (all the way back), and
a radio which is blaring Schlager, German pop songs.
'Sag mir wo die Blumen sind', 'Where have all the flowers gone'.
For the moment we can see them on the summer meadows.
Carpets of them. Feeling Angst, we sing our hearts out.
My friend just left her husband who tried to keep her locked in
and threw the key away, while I wonder whether Max will call.

6

Lucky and I. At Sint Annastrand, the Schelde 'beach'
near Antwerp. 'Smoke Gets in Your Eyes' from the loudspeakers.
The sun is gentle. Lucky is getting fat. I am 21 going onto 30.
It's a miracle that Madame let her out. Madame has a 'pension'
in the old part of town, near the *Bourse*. And a bar.
I am in the cheaper room at the back. We've become friends,
Lucky and I. She used to do the streets. Knows every trick
in the book to protect me from what she calls 'predators'.
I don't want to be protected. Tired after dancing in the Rumanian
Gipsy joint, I came back at three this morning. Slipped off my
shoes, but Lucky heard me anyway, made sure I was alone.

7

'Taivas on sininen ja valkoinen', the sky is blue and white.
Learning Finnish is impossible, but I can remember songs.
Arrived in Helsinki when the Baltic was frozen, and in August
a headline that makes everyone laugh proudly:
'Two Africans Fainted from the Heat in Oulu'. Fancy that.
It's 1957.
Camped with the bears in Karelia, learned to recite
'Little Red Riding Hood' in Finnish,
bought fresh fish in the market by the harbour,
tried to cut a chicken in half with rose shears,
getting a tan on my cousin's farm. The sauna is ready.
My brother's wedding will be soon. Must fly home.

8

My mother at the door. The party is in full swing. There
are a few boys. And my mother is at the door at eleven sharp,
dragging me out. The party is at a friend's house. Not far
from home. But Mother is 'she who will be obeyed'.
I must be home by 11.00. 'Mr Anthony's Boogie'.
I am sweating, my hair limp. Adrenalin pumping.
And my mother is at the door.
'Komm jetzt sofort hier raus!' Her face a dark cloud.
Tomorrow I'll play Beethoven for her, and Mozart.
The piano needs tuning, and my shame hangs like a cloak.

9

My brother has built a crystal radio in a cigar box.
He lets me listen to it when he feels generous of spirit.
He is my big brother. I am only small.
He listens to the American Forces Network.
I learn to say it. He puts his finger to his lips. Shhh. Don't!
or we get into heap great big trouble.
Mother at the sewing machine, my budgie on her shoulder.
They are talking to each other.

My brother says we are losing the war. My mother sings
me to sleep after she tucks the eiderdown tightly around me.
'Schlafe mein Kindchen, schlaf ein . . .'
So long as the bombers don't come. Dreams of fire.
Tomorrow I'll eat.

Feierabend

in English is something like 'closing time'. A welcome relief.
After a raucous afternoon and evening, the pub's bell
finally rings, and everyone trickles out,
often somewhat reluctantly.
And there is cleaning to be done, the wet beer rings
to be wiped off the wooden tables, the glasses stowed away,
the cash counted and the books kept. The stuff no-one
has the time to do when it's all loud voices, friendly and less
friendly ribbing, the odd overflow, hopefully in the bathroom,
rounds generously bought, free beers shamefully accepted.

My grandfather, heavy boots, coming home
from the paper mill, looked forward to his 'Feierabend',
his closing time. My mother was tired, ready to shut shop.

My brother, tired of pain, just wanted to go home.
Father was convinced the glory awaited him after hours.

Recently I felt ready for a 'closing time', sitting down,
kicking off my shoes, relaxing, letting someone else make supper.

II.

Coming Home

Madrid

It's been four long COVID years. I watch the screen on which the little plane inches along towards our destination. 'We are getting ready to land at Madrid Barajas, please return to your seats'. Barajas, the name of a village taken over by runways. There she is, grinning with affection. My old friend. I am weighed down by clothes for two seasons. Then there are the presents, of course. From Peru with love. Madrid's familiar skyline makes me feel that I am home again.

London

Can't wait to see them all. Kids, granddaughters, friends . . . We are landing. London, Heathrow. I'll be taking the train. My son will be waiting for me at Victoria Station. The man with a big neck, lots of hair and muscles looks at my cases. Travelling alone, Ma'am? 15 minutes in the 'silent car'. Small joys. I can see him now. God, Mum, what's all this? He grins and takes over. I can't believe that chaotic Victoria Station forecourt would ever turn me on. And there's the Cornish Pasty Shop. Deliciousness wafts over. So good to be home again.

Duesseldorf

We are landing at Duesseldorf. They've only got one airport. Didn't bother to name it. A small on-board case: one extra shirt and clean knickers. My brother is standing at the back of the waiting crowd, still tall. Smiles his reluctant smile. Hi, sis. Travelling light? I'll only be here for four days and sure of the climate. We are driving past my old school. It looks vaguely familiar. They built a lot, he explains, and the little trees have grown. I am home again in a melancholic way.

Lima

It's time. Lima, Peru. They've only got one airport but call it Jorge Chavez. No, not Hugo. Lima in winter. Marinated in grey. Shuffling through immigration control, like sheep being herded to the dip. Shit, where's my resident's card . . . Oh, I forgot: I have a passport now! Hope they won't open my cases full of love from London, Madrid and Duesseldorf. Husband waves. Apart from his jeans and sweater he wears one red rose and a big grin. I'm home again.

Bodies

1

Big, thin, fat, short, tall, frail, strong,
incomplete—vulnerable to destruction
from the inside out,
from the outside in.
Vehicle of consciousness, loved and hated
receiving the rejection of thoughtless comparison,
or the velvet glove of exaggerated self-love.
Bodies, the packaging that sometimes
splits right open.

2

My body. I once lost it. Melted right into
the warm and conscious stone on a Finnish island
in the summer of 1957. I remember lichen,
stone caresses, and the lightness of being.

Finding Out Where I Belong

1

After walking up, up, the mists rising
from the wetlands below made us sit
by the side of the small mountain path
and lean against our backpacks.
Sleep came easy. When we opened our eyes,
the Alpine peaks stood stark in brilliant sunlight,
throwing sharp shadows, making us gasp.
After the glory of the peaks, my insignificance
almost made me retch. I knew
I was a fly tickling the mighty rock. All the rock
had to do was shrug.

2

I had read about the sea. Had seen pictures,
of course. I had—with curious fingers—crossed
the Atlantic, plumbed the depth of the Mariana trench.
I had seen films where fishermen perished in giant waves.
When I beheld the vast and dark North Sea
for the first time, the horizon at the end of the world
took my breath away, and I wondered what kept the waves
from reaching for me.

3

A small village, pressed in between two forests,
two rivers and a lowly mountain chain. Behind
our house fields, then a mix of birches, conifers, and aspen.
When I stood on a milestone in summer, I delighted
in the wave of the wheat field. Skylarks would climb
ever higher, a cuckoo announced her home invasion,
insects buzzed in the high grasses, frogs glugged on stones
in the village brook, in the wood my steps fell soft
on moss and rotting old tree trunks. Arrows of light
cut through the green canopies. I sat, my back against
a birch, wishing for nothing.

Waltz Me Towards the Tango

Düsseldorf
Helsinki
Paris
Antwerp
Amsterdam
London. The 60s. A husband and a family.
My mother tongue goes on crutches
with a disturbed syntax,
while I am growing
into my new language
yet unformed, a toddler
that wobbles with insecure legs onto a page.

Everything is new and not that shiny.
Learning how to be a wife, soon to be a mother.
Finding out where the buses go. Living on love
and father-in-law's occasional offerings (he's got
a shop in Finsbury Park . . . food, mostly).

Liebe Mutti, Ich brauche Dich. I need you, Mum.
The telephone is expensive, letters take up to five days.
By the time they get to their destination, the news
is old. When I bring that baby home, I am sure
I'll kill him. Washing the nappies by hand,
moving my hips to the neighbour's blue beat.

I can't quite express what is in me, I don't quite
understand the laughter that follows an obvious
joke, not that the joke is at all obvious to me. I dress
like the Queen Mum at parties designed for minis or
bell-bottoms. My slow waltzes still inform my first twist,
my friends gently take the piss,
and I am not yet sure about the 'why'.

Years pass, my language is English, the learning
curve was steep, the result satisfying. Laughing about
myself comes easy, and I discover a sense of humour
that draws from a well I share in a surprising
and profound way. I read my favourites in the original.
I timidly reach out to words that might a poem make.

Life's vagaries bring me to Lima via Madrid.
My tangos are blighted by the memory of flamenco,
salsa a far cry from the Beatles,
and I am fluent in Spanish.
I am fluent in Catholic, and fluent
in Latin shoulder shrugs. I have learned to read
through superficial *amabilidad* and the every-day language
of taking oneself very seriously.

But my library, sprinkled with books
in the languages of distant planets,
is filled with pages in English, the last plank of my ship
that broke apart somewhere over the Pacific.

Sweet Ghetto

Rosh Hashanah, Eid al-Fitr, Diwali,
Weihnacht, Lughnasadh,
Blintzes, Fattoush, Luchi,
Spekulatzius, pumpkin pie . . .
Each festival superimposed
on the ones that went before.

The road less travelled by.
Wer jetzt kein Haus hat baut sich keines mehr.
Elle est retrouvée. Quoi? —L'Éternité.
We are only as blind as we want to be.

We recognize the quotes, recognize
the ritual, imagine the taste of falafel.
We know the smell, the choucroute
of Germanness, the coq-au-vin,
o là là, that leaves no doubt about Frenchness.

Callaloo that points the finger to
Jamaica, or West Africa, an exotic treat.
You smile in recognition.
Curry, basmati rice. Our mouths swim
with the saliva of expectation.

The ghetto is where they know us,
if we want to be known. It's the place
where no explanations are needed.

But you've fallen for the illusion.
The world is a big place, and you want it.
You get out.

Those who are at home where you are not
tell you theirs is the place
where you can fill your pockets
with different tunes, quotes, and choreographies.
They would have you believe that their offering
is the better bet, they have lived it, drank it,
sung it, talked it. *Our language is unique;*
it can say so much more (than yours, that's implied).

Sweet ghetto, I can't find my way back. Lost my key
on the way out, seeking what I thought
was freedom. I have just found out my new cage
is my mirage and, like Hänsel, I better stick licked-off
chicken bones through the grate or I'll be devoured.

Family Reunions

I can't remember any. Not then. Not
when I was small.
There was family, of course.
We saw each other in installments.
If at all. We were strewn all over the world,
lost to the vagaries of war and the mess
it makes of lives.
I am not even sure we liked each other enough
to wish for reunions.

Love must be nourished. Even though there may well be
moments and good reasons why you would rely
on blood ties. It is almost expected, even though
the outcome is by no means assured. Still, family
sometimes surprises even you.

In my worst teenage daughter moment
I told my mother that the people you love
are in your life because you want them to be there,
not because they're there by default.

Between Finland, the US, France, Holland,
the still United Kingdom, and Germany, between
death and destruction, family reunions
didn't exactly flourish.

Now I live about 5500 nautical miles away
from those I know I love most.

Once upon a time it was my ex-husband's
new wife who collected family and friends
with typical Greek hospitality
and bending tables every time I hit London.
He died.

I didn't

My brother said, 'Don't come. '
I didn't. Fly out to see her one last time.
My brother said, 'She doesn't know who I am'.
I figured she wouldn't know who I am either.

I had never been near the deaths of my loved ones.
I think I avoided the grief.
I had lost them already.
Or so I'd thought.
Or so I'd hoped?
I had just picked up my children from school.
My brother called, 'She's gone'.
I could hear his utter disbelief.
His voice choking in watery phlegm.

And suddenly I felt empty, abandoned,
a forlorn child in a big world,
a woman without substance,
homeless.

And suddenly my losses multiplied,
and all the tears I'd never shed
filled a salty ocean of grief and guilt.

And suddenly I was there with her, wrestling
with her demons. I wondered whether
I would have recognized her.
My father had been a dark-blue, life-size remake
in a life-size box, vaguely reminding me
of the man who held open his arms when
I came flying.

Three days to dying.
Three days of longing.

Three days of holding on.
Perhaps . . .
But I didn't.
I didn't. Fly out to see her one last time.
Leave everything and hurry to see her and let her touch me
one last time, let her know I cared enough.
To tell her one more time 'I love you, Mum',
tell her one more time 'I am strong
because you made me so'.
Thank her one more time for
giving me her life.

Discontent

Early spring in the subtropics
make me wish for that tree,
fat with apple blossoms,
a host of humming
small folk pollinating
and feasting.

Closing my eyes, I smell
again the freshness
of a cool April morning,
able to call up the seduction
of feathery blossom fingers
on my cheeks.

Would there be felicity
without caressing
losses and ignoring gains,
exalting crystalized narcissus
early March in the north of the North
while succumbing to the exotic wiles
of the glorious cantuta.

Now in the late years of my life
I wish for an Indian summer
instead of a winter of discontent.

Damage Control

Four damaged dolls and I
lived in my house.
My mother knew, but
I failed to find my affliction.

There were five damaged
lovers in my life. I failed to see
how love could have
cut them so deeply.

My children brought each
a piece of me into this world
and, in despair, changed into toads.

I often squat in the mud by the pond
learning a new way to speak,
especially with my daughters.

Friends

There are so many kinds of awful friends,
the kind that hug, and smile, and wave
as long as you are not too shiny
in their eyes.

—Oh, daaaahling, you look gorgeous!
—Does she not?
When you meet jogging, sweating, and in leggings
that have seen better days . . .
But there are ways.

You snagged that job, you're on TV,
your book is out, your daughter's PhD.
The only way to beat them
is to beat them good
to make them meek, and mean,
and shut their gob.

When they go pale, a little green
around the gills,
you won the 'war' you did not seek
against ill will.

Counting Sheep

I am trying to recite my mantra:
'aum manu padme hum'. It's just long enough
to force some concentration and cheat my
brain into believing that getting it right
is all it needs to agonize about. I sleep

until that aging bladder wants to be emptied.
After feet on cold floor, broadening hips knocking
the chest of drawers again, I worry that
I might have woken my partner, but daring
to look in his direction I cannot make out movement
or accusation. My brain lights up and gets to work,

making lists of everything that might be useful
for a little panic. Will I remember that first line
of my just conceived poem tomorrow? Did I put
some beers in the fridge to be cold tomorrow?
Perhaps I ought to write to my bank first thing or they
block my account! Where will my friend and I have lunch
tomorrow? (Why on earth should that make me worry . . .)
If the lift doesn't work, I'll have to climb six floors tomorrow.
When was that funeral—should I have gone?
Do we have onions?

Sleep finally finds me again 15 minutes before
my body knows it's time to make breakfast.

Aum Manu Padme Hum

It's not working. Have sweated
over it. Like a poor soul at heaven's door
with a sledgehammer.

The others seem to be chosen. Golden
bridges, starlight, angels . . . All I ever
see is Marga's buttocks.
Aum. Ohm. Oooomygawd.

Hum. I shift from lotus. My knees
hurt. My mind wanders. I kick the waves
walking along that North Sea island
beach. The waves eat my feet. Not
in an angry way. I look down at
the stumps where my feet used
to be and hop through the dry sand.

My hands in the pockets of the
too large shorts my brother lent
me. I need them for balance,
but the pockets hold them fast
with black rubber teeth. I fall
into one of those rock pools

where a transparent thing with legs
and big eyes is soon eating my thighs.
Takes big bites. I am relieved there
is no pain. The sun burns the top
of my scalp. Five vultures shift
from one foot to the other in ennui,
sure that I'll give in soon. I can read
their minds. A seagull startles me.
Tries to peck at my right eye.

The tide is going out. My thighs
are numb. A voice gently asks me to open
my eyes. No way. That seagull isn't very far.

Should You Not Recognize Me,
How Could I Explain Myself to You?

I fear you have pegged me with your expectation,
have created me in the image
someone prepared for you.
If all you can see
is black and white, look again.
Search for colour within
colour, shape within shapes.
Within.

Stay for a while, calm, open your heart
and your mind.
Listen.
I may not be what you expected,
but I can give you peace.

The Day I Stopped Reading the News

I smiled. My childhood woodlands
before me, I smelled wild mushrooms.
Eyes closed, my skin warmed
in the sun of summers past,
when the skylark rose
trilling its mating song.

The place that had been a black cave
of shrilling pain, little claws scratching
their blood marks into my flesh,
the deep pool where tentacles
pulled me into its depth, opened
instead to a forest where sunbeams danced
on the wings of tiny creatures
that carried joy.

Music

1

Special earphones brought me a priceless gift.
They let me hear the higher frequencies again
and with them the full range of Kiri Te Kanawa's gentle soprano.

2

Easter. I am not a believer, but then there is Bach.
There is *'Ach, Golgathata'* and
'Wir setzen uns mit Tränen nieder',
the well of ache, the death of love,
the betrayal with a kiss, the sudden absence of laughter.
The hot pain of a failure, and the knowledge
that a hungry black hole had opened,
devouring what I thought we'd built.

3

Music breaks locks to doors I can no longer see.
My new-found clarity of hearing
makes me bee-like.
I flit from E major to G minor,
from Baroque trumpets to the Mariachi
torturing the instrument with gusto,
take a crazy dip into The Chieftains, Enya, Adiemus and
Leonard Cohen's baritone-voice poetry of spirit and sex,
Joni Mitchell, the Carpenters, Vivaldi, Mahler, Miles Davis,
Joaquín Rodrigo, Don McLean, Roy Orbison . . . I am drunk.

4

I swing from memories of a marriage on a fakir's bed
to the delight of holding my babies,
indulging them—just one more, Mum—
with 'Teddy Bear's Picnic'.
Their soft, just bathed, shining faces sleepy
in the yellow light of the bedside lamp.

5

I lost 'Stairways to Heaven' when my kids spirited
all my Led Zeppelin albums into their LP collections
before complaining that mine contained nothing of interest.
They, in turn, gave me gifts of immense value.
'We will we will rock you . . .'

6

"There ain't no cure for love"

Gravity

I remember a time
when nothing could keep me from
floating, especially when I was in love. I'd rise
easily into the clouds and rest
in their fluffiness.
Since then, earth's gravity
has increased.
Or, while I wasn't watching
I may have changed planet.
I fight the pressure
every day.
Getting out of bed
I seem to turn
into a heavy sack
of flesh and bones. Every time
I get up from my chair I weigh more.
Climbing the steps
out of the pool
my specific weight
increases to that of iron.
Even my brain has shrunk
into itself, my will is defeated,
my powers of observation limp.
Spiders walk across my eyes,
bees buzz in my ear canal,
algae and dry moss fill
empty spaces
where only yesterday
my poems grew.
Mornings shiver me and
evenings leave me shrivelled.
My steps are smaller now, hesitant,
and the heart is confused,
shaky and indecisive.

I Am Tired of Being Tired

The lethargy struck together with the monster virus.
When the worst of the coughing was over, when the fever
had left, when I could breathe freely again, I thought
I could pick up my life where I left off.
Instead, there was total fatigue. Brain fog.
Too tired to think.
Too tired to plan a future.
Too tired to write.
Too tired to smile.
Too tired to dream.
Too tired to be afraid.
Too tired to hate.
This poem doesn't like to be written.
My fight no longer wants to be fought.
Climate crisis? Let it happen. The latest news? Who cares
about Ukraine. Trump? There is a faint echo of outrage.
White supremacists? A discreet wake-up call but not enough
right now. The UK prime minister is an idiot?
They all knew that when they voted for him.
Every day seems an effort, life
itself bends under the load of its weight.
Tired words stretch like bubble gum.
Would I be a hibernating bear, safe in the knowledge
that nothing was asked of me but sleep.

How to Prepare for My Final Flight

First, let me fly. Ideally my hand in your hand,
one more time giving me warmth.
My eyes fading into the cool blue pools of yours.
Your kiss and the promise that you won't be long.

Still, I have a feeling that time is relative where I am going.
We'll not be discussing this, however.
At least not now.
I'll be taking my backpack and move over that eternal line.
Will the weight be lighter now?
Moving one waft at the time.
(I suppose I'll be wafting—it's not American football.)

As you know, I don't believe in the god the church made,
but I wouldn't mind a bit of singing.
There was the one song at my grandfather's
funeral, but that's in German and only works
if you understand the words.
It's about going home after finishing work.
My grandfather was a working man who wore
working man's boots. I can still hear his heavy, tired tread
on the wooden steps of their little house.

So you chose your favourite, Janet Baker,
even though I am telling you that Maria Ewing would do.
Still, this is your party.

Invite you best friends but try and love some of mine too.
There will be a few who would like to listen to the arias.

Once you have my ashes in a box
(you won't sink so low as to put them
into a personalized urn), promise me to take them
to the forest—any forest—to become perhaps a *sumaumeira*
in our piece of the rainforest in Peru,
a pine in the Spanish sierra, or perhaps a birch in Finland
or the German Alps. I would very much want
what stays behind to become a tree.

However, as I said, it's not my party.
I would love to be tall and gorgeous, and able give you shade.

Remembering Where I Came From

The genetic basis of air-breathing and limb movement was already established in our fish ancestor 50 million years earlier, according to a recent genome mapping of primitive fish. The new study changes our understanding of a key milestone in our own evolutionary history.

And at the beginning were vats of warm, slimy mud
fed by steam heated by volcanoes.
Then there were oceans.

In my fever dream I am in the kelp forests
and contemplate the sunlight
filtering through green . . . and brown.

In the coral reefs I hunt, and learn from
the stories told by those who have always
been there: watching, listening, giving shelter.

I look up and see the manta rays pass overhead,
undulating big wings, tails moving gently, an army
that darkens my world when it passes.

Like the manta rays, I feel my power when I break through
to take to the air, and something whispers in my blood:
'One day air will be all you have'.

A White Sheet of Paper

I contemplate
the white rectangle
of paper on which
nothing is written.
It is in abeyance.

There shall be no
budding of words,
no binding
of seeds to what seems
their future.

Free

to shift essence,
gather resonances.

Wraiths born
remain
untold.

A white sheet of paper.
A gateway.

Bless the Broken Things

1

The cuckoo clock fell.
I became a clock builder.
The cuckoo's voice had broken.
I learned how to heal a four-year-old heart.

2

Christmas again.
Dolls disappeared.
They came back made whole.
I had loved them broken.

3

Pregnant again,
forgot about unslept nights,
sore breasts and haemorrhoids.
Baby changed her mind.
The doctor says she was broken.

4

Alone again.
He brought her home,
I made her bed to stay the night.
When I found out the truth,
something inside me broke.

5

In Japan they mend broken things
with gold. The former fault lines become works of art
reminding me of the exquisite lines in the faces
of those who have healed.

A No-Time

No crystals in this winter that falls upon us
with stealth. Music of the spider harps
rolling off softly rotting leaves. Sickness,
melancholy and anger fuse to build barriers
against a youth that lacks its usual bluster.

A fading day without the glow of heavenly furnaces,
the once rolling waves stilled, a tumultuous silence
submerging the shore inch by sodden inch.

Gaia is dimming. The wake-up calls
are more frequent now: Fire, water, heat,
molten lava and a tiny killer.

Blue

Read somewhere on the Internet:
[. . .] ancient languages didn't have a word for blue—not Greek, not Chinese, not Japanese, not Hebrew. And without a word for the color, there is evidence that they may not have seen it at all [. . .]

Wine-dark seas, violet sheep, green honey.
The poet can evoke at will,
let us see what Homer saw.
If we can't witness with a word
we are not able to know.

So feed the words to the roaring silence.
Let us un-know, un-fear, un-dread,
un-do the knots we have tied so tight
that they keep us packaged the way
a spider keeps its prey.

I Wonder

where the hole goes when it's closed,
the space which you displaced by living,
the knot once it's untied,
the love when it no longer fills me.

Friday Night Binge in the City of London

His big sweaty palm leaves a mark.
She barely notices his touch.
She's on her fifth Rum and Coke
Rum to get that tension down,
Coke to keep her standing.
Old-fashioned drink but who
cares and she doesn't do stuff.

He wishes for a large ungulate
and a shiny armour.
It's a sweet summer night and the
'Slug and Lettuce' is full. He gets
waylaid by shiny things.
It's so inevitable.

She's switches to vodka orange.
Her wings feel wooden.
Her laughter sounds shriller.
Her standing becomes erratic.
His kisses taste of brass.
Strange.
She thought he was in equities.
When she slides into fetal position
by the green container
the trombone falls from his hands.
Don't touch
my soul.

Cumbrian Summer

The mudroom. Wildflowers on the kitchen table.
Big eiderdowns in which I could disappear.
Mother and I played hide-and-seek
during that last summer,
before her hair fell out.

We ran through oak woodland
and pretended to fish in the tarns.

Father couldn't come, she said.
Sometimes she'd sit by the window
looking out at nothing.

Those were the afternoons
when I professed to read,
with deep interest, my book
on English wildflowers.
With illustrations.

In London, on a drip
of lifesaving poison,
she smiled at the memory.
And the silence
was too loud.

Letter to Angst

It's not as though
I'm missing you. In fact
I am so very glad we are
no longer travelling companions.
I don't want to be unkind,
but you have been my albatross,
an aliquant in my potential for happiness,
a fly in the ointment which ought to have
lubricated my Ferris wheel,
greased the cogs that moved my clockworks,
been rubbed into my aching wings.

Orion is my witness, the Hunter's Moon
my mother confessor. In fact, the
Milky Way used ear plugs when I sat
on that plastic boulder
howling you into the night.

My secret burden, I am glad you jumped ship
somewhere between Berlin and the Pleiades.
Wherever you hang out or on, be kind.
Go easy on the hosts that give you life.

Spurned

She put her unspent love into a cardboard box,
added a few choice curses and shut the lid.
Firmly.

He hadn't even seen her when he nearly bumped
into her on his breathless trajectory
towards the long-haired blonde, long-legged tanned,
slim-waisted, soft-lipped, fake Barbie.

May her bed become infested with bedbugs,
may her legs and armpits grow untameable,
shaggy undergrowth, may her hair fall out in clumps,
her teeth rot to black stumps, her lips reduce to two
thin slices; better still, may her face fall off.
May their children be fat, stupid, snotty and
may his penis hurt when they make love.

She then dropped the cardboard box
into the flames of the fireplace,
fearing she may open it one day and forgive.

When It's All Over

Perhaps mountains still echo our voices—
at least a whisper of the banter during the hike,
moments of fear on the sheer rock side,
a soft 'ah' or 'oh' of human wonder
at the majesty of the unforgiving peaks.

Water may still remember our form,
the caresses when it opened to let us in,
then closed after we passed.
An ephemeral reminder of what was solid once.

Air formerly made room for us, entered us,
only to leave again bearing a souvenir of our DNA.
A whiff of particulates of skin and laughter,
of young witches dancing on soft grass in the hollow.

Alien archaeologists may find fossils of a jawbone here,
a femur there, a child's skeleton perfectly preserved
in post-apocalyptic mud. How will they know us?

Our poems carried on the wind, storms lifted
the crescendos of our most passionate symphonies,
pompous oratory hung from pillars left standing
after giant waves thundered in and flushed sand,
plastic, concrete, and stone, perhaps
exposing two lovers embracing,
bone on brittle bone.

Where Poems Live

Look for the spaces between words,
the hand cupped to receive water,
find the question without answers
or the great, ecliptic circle,
seemingly eternal and reliable, but there are doubts.
Then there is the hunger in your eyes,
the crumpled sheets of a lovers' bed,
the musty smell of sweat and sex,
the sunny green pushing through spring leaves in a glen,
the flowers of knotweed.
Fresh croissants and éclairs from Fouquet's
on the Champs Elysées, the first log fire
of an early autumn evening,
woodsmoke pushed down by a gentle breeze,
freshly cut grass, petrichor of course,
and watering a dry lawn
after a long, hot August day.

That brings me to the seconds
between lightning and thunder,
and bodyless presences
when the clock strikes three am.
Then think of dark eddies in the brook
under the willow and add a Nyad or two.
Oh, I could go on, as could you.
But this will do for now and anyone who asked.

Yin and Yang

Joyful equilibrium
Connect to your power
Move the world
She, them, their and his
Dance power
Balance life forces
Use the might of a spider yarn

time somewhere

sunflowers in the headlights
giving themselves to the storm,
black clouds leave windmills
inert, the canal heaves and blubs,
its concrete prison aches
under the weight of lust,
last rays on a golden
lower-Rhine wheat field,
black birds cleaning up
before morning, poplars
whisper and bend,
plane trees without leaves,
their naked trunks defenseless.
the rain-men watch,
a secret service of observers
distilled into green,
winter shower leaves
crystals, pearls, and red claws,
the sheep are in revolt.
a brown crumpled old
dry leaf perches delicately
on a web of weary branches
promise of another winter.
sand clouds spook a herd
of wild horses, the mad
fall-girl saves crumpled fingers
for when next a time comes
for bells and hosts of pollinators.

urban wilderness

an alien body kept alive by tubes,
the neighbour's blue beat,
hanging out the washing
when the moon was full,
wallpaper maps of years,
other voices, hardships.
flowers under stripes.
steaming,
plastering
big wooden board.
a small voice from the nursery window.
pink roses sprayed white.
set for an advertising video
or a pop promotion.
grass so high I lost my child.
almost.
weeping willow
over my baby's pram,
moving leaves
play a visual melody.
magpies pick out eyes.

Recipe for Wellness

I recommend a pinch of self-mockery,
and two teaspoons full of shoulder shrugs
because, after all, there isn't much you can do.
Add a cup full of hilarity and two units
of friendship. Let it brew and pour in laughter—
as much as the bowl will hold—wrap it all
in unconditional love. Forgetting is not part of this recipe,
but top your mixture with a generous dollop of forgiveness.
Take this at least five times a day then lie back,
relax, and have a glass of Champagne.

Sighting of the Unicorn

Some said they saw it all.
Others came from the mist
and heard the stories
told by those who hadn't really been there.
They were unanimous:

It had risen from the snow,
had leaped from the underbrush,
rushed towards the king's men,
horn lowered it had skewered the wolf,
had turned from white to blue
when the moon came up,
it had whinnied with triumph
and melted into the fog.
They had seen it.
It had been a hoax.

As time passed, the unicorn deniers
and the believers escalated their
differences until war became inevitable.
The cause forgotten as soon pure hate
made the men and women lower their lances.

Somewhere, Moon Time

Wolves howling, snows drifting,
blizzards covering field and brush. A muzzle
opens, fangs glistening in the white light,
an echo in the woods. Fine droplets arc
from the flews. It's almost upon you.
Wolf Moon.

Cabins, pathways, bushes indistinct,
flowing into each other under thick
eiderdowns of heavy whiteness.
No animal stirs, the hunter asleep,
the children dream of food.
Hunger Moon.

The tinkle of water on ice, slush
and suction on muddy fields,
crusts on refrozen snow, crows
alighting, leaving their intoeing
spoors. Hope for bird song.
Crow Moon.

Cowslip, hyacinth, lilac, bluet.
First spring greens unfolding
from naked branches, blackened earth.
Tadpoles socialize in the shallow pond,
Sudden frost only threatens.
Pink Moon.

Shadbush, catalpa, and dogwood,
bees hum between branches
of rhododendrons and the first
mountain laurel, buzz in and out
of pink azaleas. Time for planting.

Flower Moon.
Nights are sweet. Thieves abound.
Birds, slugs, snails move in to harvest
young leaves. Strawberries
fail to hide undercover of green.
Picked for midsummer's day.
Strawberry Moon.

Prussian, indigo, midnight blue,
black. July storms, racing clouds
slashed, flattened wheat fields.
Raindrops the size of hummingbird eggs.
Deer retreat into the woods.
Thunder Moon.

The white sturgeon takes the bait,
the horizons glow crimson, August hazes
drift across water. The winds
of the end of summer.
Make haste.
Red Moon.

Bring in the corn. Store squash,
pumpkins, beans, and rice, work late
by the light of the moon. Shoulder
the burden of obligation, prepare
for the earth's big sleep.
Harvest Moon.

Stalk patiently, the deer are fat.
Light the smokestack. Your mount
takes the hedges in pursuit of the fox,
the dachshund follows the badger.
The end of fall is unforgiving.
Hunter's Moon.

The beavers are making sure their lodges
are secured, check on their dams,
add one or two. Set your trap.
A beaver hat will see you through
the worst of winter.
Beaver Moon.

Longest nights, the big sleep.
Light the fire, cut the wood,
protect your stores from furry robbers,
sit with a mulled wine, leaf through
a book of poetry.
Cold Moon.

On the Cusp

It's hard to wait. You expect so much, and your mum
has it all. She's got Dad, she's got the dresses,
the shoes, the lipstick . . . and when she puts you to bed
at night before going out she smells of forbidden things.

And now you're 12. You just looked and saw your potential.
You understood your power. And you tried on you sister's
red dress. Those shoulders . . . yes. Just right. A little blusher,
Mum's lipstick. Tame that hair with gel.

When you look again you have a premonition
of what lies in wait for young women and become quiet.
While remaining determined, you have a moment of doubt.
You don't know yet that one day the dress will have to come off.

The Magic of the Word, or the Blind Girl Reads Braille

There is a world under your fingertips.
There are words that tell you about worlds
under fingertips.

And you shut your eyes—even though what they can't see
doesn't distract you—just to feel your way across
Samarkand, the Silk Road, the Gobi Desert, climb Machu Picchu,
and meet fellow travellers.

There is a world under your fingertips,
and from deep inside yourself you reach out to the green
of emeralds, the stern, bearded sheiks, and daring maidens.
You get up awkwardly onto a camel,
or you spend the rest of the afternoon
in a forest that smells of pine, moss, and decay.
You wonder about 'green' . . .

A rumor has it that Tiresias was blinded by Athena
after he saw her bathing.
What did you see?

There is a world under your fingertips,
and now you know that Schopenhauer was wrong.
You can transcend the everyday point of view
because you are not waylaid by shiny things.

Old Knowledge

Palm fronds in the chubby hands
of kids in white vestments.
Exotic leaves
meant to protect me from the northern dark.

My husband's sister
pins the nazar to my children's vests.
Warding off
the evil eye.

Voices cross the world.
Hand of Fatima.
Whisper.

The ofuda is pretty, I tell
my Japanese neighbour.
She attaches a piece
of decorated wood
to my door.

The wind chimes tinkle icicles.
Frozen hawthorn.

Make me a cross
from the rowan tree.
Tie it with a red ribbon.

Celtic woman made from rowan.
Runes carved from rowan.
Thor saved by the rowan.
Each berry a pentagram.

Our dead circle the house
carolling songs of the roots.

no way out

There was the treatment centre.
The others.
The drugs.
The drugs.
The drugs.
They took away
the weight of obligation.

They said she was getting better and
she watched the baby grow,
thinking of endless years of boredom before her.
She cleaned the house, made the beds.
Opened the door to her mother-in-law
whose smile was too sweet and forgiving.
She acquiesced.
The second baby was a girl.

That day he came home from the office
early, cut her down gently.

Nightcall

when night presses down
and muffles all sound
when your wings are weary
and you would be chained
                        call me

when the chirpy voices
of girls under streetlights
mute slowly in distended mist
eyes drowned by indifference
                        I'll be waiting

when the wavelets stop lapping
and the fish go deep
when you don't ask
because you no longer want to know
                        I'll have the answers

when you drown in unmadeness
spooked by hyaline skin
lost in amorphous potential
greeting your everywhereanytime
                        I'll unfold with you

My Friend in Meth

Curious to know where everyone
flows to with such eager determination.
Sirens squealing.
Red and blue lights.

Without hurry I amble
to the front.

Something that used to be human
lies in the dirty slush
where a pristine white
sheet of snow fell only minutes ago.
The face black pulp. Foetal position.
Eating the earth.

I know that hat.
Always full of those fresh flowers
Beth never forgot to steal
when she needed an upper.

Portent

The pharaoh's dream:
seven ears of corn
blasted by the east wind.

Moses summons the east wind
to bring the locusts
and to part the Red Sea.

The east wind.
Destruction of the wicked
called forth by God himself.

Mary Poppins arrives
carried by the east wind
and will stay
"until the wind changes."

Sherlock: "There's an east wind coming, Watson."
"You left the East Wind to me," said Gimli,
"but I will say naught of it."
"That is as it should be," says Aragorn.
"In Minas Tirith they endure the East Wind,
but they do not ask it for tidings . . ."

In 'Bleak House', Mr Jarndyce:
"I am always conscious of an uncomfortable
sensation now and then
when the wind is blowing in the east."

Genghis Khan: the east wind
that changed the map of the world.

The Chulel*

> *The Mexican shamans call the soul a 'chulel',
> and according to them everything has a chulel.*

The thirteen layers of each *chulel*
must be cared for. Shamans know
what to do when you knock
one layer out of whack.
Sacrifice a hen.
Drink Coca-cola.

Chuleles don't live
on the surface of the earth.
That's just a game of perception,
trickery, illusion.

You find heaven in caves
and on mountaintops.
The dead and the saints
live in the world of dreams.

Sing, dance, drink, write poetry, weave . . .
Make God think that he did well.
Anything to prevent Him from thinking
He must start all over again.

The Prophet's Vision

Wailers and howlers
wolves and hyenas.
A place of rest for the screech owl.
Specter.
Lilith flies by night.

Shaggy beasts take up their abode
in the powerful realm:

And the satyr shall cry to its fellow,
half goat and half man,
and Rome shall fall.

Her nobles shall be no more,
nor shall kings be proclaimed there,
all her princes are gone. Her castles
shall be overgrown with thorns,
her fortresses with thistles and briers.

Sunsets on Mars Are Blue

Scientists have just possibly found a medicine
that slows the development of Alzheimer's.
They are working on a vaccine against HIV.
Astronomers capture radio signals
from a distant galaxy.
The Russians are getting a space craft ready
on a rocket of some major proportions
to rescue two astronauts from the stricken
space station. SpaceX plans to use the Starship
to fly a Japanese businessman around the moon.
Oh, and several artists too. Wonder who.
We'll soon be sending settlers to Mars.
They'll be sitting on their porches contemplating
the Martian sunsets.
Meanwhile, concerned citizens are afraid of people
who doubt the gender they were assigned at birth,
afraid of people who love
their own gender.
Deny that slaves ever existed.
Burn books.
Idolize the Golden Calf and then some.
The honorable justices of their so-called Supreme Court
are denying women control of their bodies
and possibly would like, as a next step,
to forge a bond with the clergy of Iran who condemn
to death by hanging any woman who shows her hair,
or with Afghanistan's Taliban
who deny women the right to education,
independent movement, and even Kabul's
female mannequins are masked and hooded.
While sunsets on Mars are Blue.

Tumble

Meriam Webster:

a: to fall suddenly and helplessly

Your sphincter relaxes.
it only takes seconds, but you know
that you might break something.
Even your neck
If encased in a metal suit, you may shrivel
in it slowly like a dead plum.
Pruning.
Nobody will hear your cries
for help, only your own ears.
Your armour rusts.
Eventually it will disintegrate
and metal will mix with
your biodegradables.
Nature will reclaim it all.

b: to suffer a sudden downfall, overthrow, or defeat

They attacked you from behind.
You had set your sights on winning
the battle.
There were those who disagreed.
You first made concessions,
then you attacked.
Your allies left your flanks and back
open for the others' lances to knock
you off your horse.
You fell, an armoured beetle,
couldn't turn yourself around.
The new king left you to rot.

c: to decline suddenly and sharply

Your time has come.
Your breath is laboured.
The pain in your chest is unexpected.
You cease.

What Doesn't Kill You . . .

Begins as innocence, not being smart
enough to know it hurts to be blue in a red world.
As the man says: Happiness is being too stupid to know
what to worry about.

Bless those who get crushed because Phoenix rises.
Forged in fire, the insurrectionists:
Government mandates? No way.
Eating animals? Not anymore.
Polluting our drinking water? Bastards.
Eating plastic bread? Not us.
Glyphosate on our lettuce? Don't get me started.
Little kids digging for lithium?
Africa a dumping ground for our old computers?
Deforestation and burning the Amazon?
There is a long and varied 'et cetera'.

The new rebels are different, scorned
by those who march in step. Laughed at by their peers,
punished by teachers, parents, employers, their governments . . .
Broken and remade with their first mutiny, reclaiming the truth,
marching for peace, environment, against racism.
Mention a good cause and they'll be there with you.
Anyone old enough to remember Greenham Common?
It's not something that started today.
Like sex, it was invented a while back.
Heard of the suffragettes?

Once you've been shoved out into the cold by those
who are supposed to protect you, a little rebellion is
all in a day's work. Giving politicians the mental finger,
reading their lies, being prodded, and spat at
for your pains is akin to daily bread.

Those too cowardly to leave the well-trodden path
always have the courage to mock those
who make them feel uncomfortable.
But every day the army of non-conformists grows.
Soon they will be the majority.
Let them stay kind.

Comfort from the Birds

> *Frida Kahlo's father was born in Germany. He lived, married, and photographed in Mexico. He gave Frida her surname as well as five parrots to keep her company. She painted herself with four of them.*

Ja, Mädchen, my girl, I know. Come, *venga,*
a present for you.
Pain. Constant. *Papá los sabe,* he knows.
When I am in need, he is there for me. Even when Diego
doesn't care too much.
Father is my healer.
Qué hay, Papá, what do you have for me?
Warte, wait, Fridalein.

Five *bunte* parrots. Colourful.
All talk at the same time. A mix of German
and Spanish. They make me laugh.
Papá is a genius. How I love him.
Diego is sex, my father is love and my cushion
when the pain gets *demasiado*. Too much.
He calls me his little Frida.

When I hold a parrot, I feel his solid little body,
silky, warm, feather-covered, heart beating. Head to one side
he sees me. He says *'Hola Frida'*. He doesn't
judge. *Qué bellos son,* how beautiful their colours.
One flies off, never comes back.
Parrot, I mourn your loss but envy
your freedom. *Cuidate, mi amor.*
Take care.

Just in case another follows the call,
I paint *mis amigos* together with me.
Los loros que me dio mi Papi. The parrots
my father gave me to keep me sane.

Far Away from Cell Phone Antennae

Toads drum, calling
the rain which soon falls
on corrugated metal roofs,
drowning all other sound.
The jungle floor slippery as soap.
Semi-darkness breathes
between the giant leaves of ur-trees,
tattered shreds of white fog
drift across the lake.

Slowly the rain gives in. Again
voices shriek, clamour, whoop, chirp.
Scorpions scuttle from their nests,
birds swoop for a last catch.
Then night falls softly, while the moon
breaks into shimmering pieces
which caper across the waters.

About the Author

"If I didn't write, especially poetry, I'd probably be quite mute in five languages or, more likely, I'd implode. While my heart occasionally rummages in German, my mouth speaks Spanish, my spirit is playing in English, and I even have to look up the occasional French or Dutch word."

A German-born UK national, Rose Mary Boehm lives and works in Lima, Peru. Author of two novels and *Tangents,* a full-length poetry collection published in the UK in 2010/2011, she has had work widely published in US poetry journals (online and print). She was three times winner of the now defunct *Goodreads* monthly competition and has twice been nominated for a Pushcart. Her latest five poetry collections: *From the Ruhr to Somewhere Near Dresden 1939–1949: A Child's Journey* (Kelsay Books, 2016); *Peru Blues or Lady Gaga Won't Be Back* (Kelsay Books, 2017); *The Rain Girl* (Chaffinch Press, Ireland, 2020); *Do Oceans Have Underwater Borders?* (Kelsay Books, 2022); *Whistling in the Dark* (Cyberwit 2022), and *Saudade* (Kelsay Books, 2022).

Find out more about the author and her work on her website:
www.rose-mary-boehm-poet.com

www.ingramcontent.com/pod-product-compliance
Lightning Source LLC
Chambersburg PA
CBHW022126160426
43197CB00009B/1164